WHAT THOUGH THE FIELD BE LOST

WHAT THOUGH THE FIELD BE LOST

Christopher Kempf　　*Poems*

Louisiana State University Press

Baton Rouge

Published by Louisiana State University Press
www.lsupress.org

LSU Press Paperback Original

Designer: Laura Roubique Gleason
Typefaces: Whitman, text; AGrotesk and Tribute, display

Library of Congress Cataloging-in-Publication Data

Names: Kempf, Christopher, author.
Title: What though the field be lost : poems / Christopher Kempf.
Description: Baton Rouge : Louisiana State University Press, [2021] | Includes
   bibliographical references.
Identifiers: LCCN 2020026097 (print) | LCCN 2020026098 (ebook) | ISBN 978-0-
   8071-7363-3 (paperback) | ISBN 978-0-8071-7510-1 (pdf) | ISBN 978-0-8071-7511-8
   (epub)
Subjects: LCGFT: Poetry.
Classification: LCC PS3611.E5327 W48 2021 (print) | LCC PS3611.E5327 (ebook) |
   DDC 811/.6—dc23
LC record available at https://lccn.loc.gov/2020026097
LC ebook record available at https://lccn.loc.gov/2020026098

for Corey

For the body is not one member, but many. If the foot shall say, "Because I am not the hand, I am not of the body," is it therefore not of the body? And if the ear shall say, "Because I am not the eye, I am not of the body," is it therefore not of the body? If the whole body were an eye, where were the hearing? If the whole were hearing, where were the smelling? But now hath God set the members every one of them in the body, as it hath pleased him. And if they were all one member, where were the body? But now are they many members, yet but one body.

—1 Corinthians 12:14–20

Contents

WHAT
THOUGH
THE FIELD
BE LOST

National Anthem

If, then, a country could be saved, may we
all be its pulse & schematics. May our flags
kneel for us. May nothing reign. May *one day*
mean Tuesday, & may our planes on alert
over Khost & Riyadh whisper love songs
to the canyons beneath them. May weddings
go on for months. May guns gather bullets
back into themselves like fishing line. If
a country could be saved, could wave lagoons
too be a part of it? Could slot machines?
Could a country be lifted like a god?
If Modesto comes back, could Saturday night
we drive T-Birds to the Wolfman? May
dawn's early light lacquer our faces. May
Huck & Jim — May group text — Let every
coal seam spit back its dead. Let the many
of us be one, the one be numerous
& mongrel. Imagine *spangled* — & may
each of our stadiums smolder. May marching
bands dazzle & thrall us, *their drums like war*
no one will remark, their winds & brasses
forming the tightest of scripts. The seamstress,
we know—age 13—who dyed the cotton
& cut the starlight in the flag Francis Scott
hailed was a servant girl, Grace Wisher. May
we, in the poem of our country, be such
exquisite stitchwork. May *synecdoche*
mean "fruited plain." "Beautiful river." In
that country, nuke silos swallow missiles
down like hot dogs. In that country, cop cars
flip Snapples to day laborers. May stars
blaze. May landfills flower & hum. May one
by one we gather, then, in the swollen fields
of our republic, above us the rockets'
red glare growing faint, some praise-song
swept upon us utterly, like a wind. *May we*
we will say—which will, one day, become us.

Remembrance Day

       Improper, though, the part
of us that wants a body here. Re-
                        memor—"mindful"
   actually, the Latin is
                  incontrovertible. We want
a resurrection. Want
    membre, perhaps—from "meat"
            or "flesh." Isn't memory,
     the argument goes, our most magnificent
of surgeries? The soldiers—some of them,

   no doubt, for ancestors, others
              the spectacle—execute (all
  together, the gray
               & blue) their about-face
onto Lincoln Street, each group's
     parade sergeant swinging
        his replica cutlass, the sidewalks
  of Gettysburg thick with tourists.
                  Townie children
wave little American flags. Vast coolers
     shimmer with pops. We want

   the 19th century again—
our men returned to us, the country's
          one body bandaged together
with the neat sutures of Law. The long column

          of reenactors—also
fifes & buglers, boys
  with wheelbarrows full of horse shit—stretches
        through town to our street
of dive bars & t-shirt vendors.
       McClellan,
     raised, sips Fireball. Shaw's
black regiment relays a fishbowl
    to Stuart's Virginians. Artillery

Punches slosh. Wine
coolers. Juleps. The truces

of old, of course, came too
with their great trayfulls of cocktails.
At Culp's Hill,
surgeons administered whiskey—it was
my backyard, the tours will tell you, the Rebels
& Yanks beside each other
in the hospital barns—before
their procedures, bit
tightened in the soldiers' mouths.
Isn't memory,

more rightly, the pile of shinbones
in the cutting room bucket? One
leg leveled off
at the hip. Isn't it
the South's stunned body they went back
to & flew their bitterness
over? Hoses.
Affidavits. In
Reconstruction Texas, some men
walked another man through town—the crowd
we know from photographs, his scaffolding
like a float—& before
they burned him ran irons
through his feet & windpipe. Isn't this
our country? From
"flesh." From
a past we imagine
could have been—can you
believe that?—one
once.
Tecumseh Sherman
drinks High Life at a picnic table.

He is a roofer from Knoxville.

Michaux State Forest, New Year's

We run the *kókúku* trail (translation—
snow owl, in late-American) alone
this morning, its strict, midwinter alders
dark against the snowfall, its flocks of crows
shrieking as we pass. & as for the river—
there is a river. & as for those vast
accumulations of gasses—& as,
too, for the Fords & Hyundais, & the flows
of copper from Chile to Santa Cruz
& the migrant workers of Sri Lanka
scaling their towers in Dubai—that will,
some evening, rear up & expunge us,
yes, Corey & I can almost imagine
ourselves last here, some sole surviving pair
of scavengers ventured forth for water
& shelter, as surely it will be, we
accept now, those new years the planet—poor
rock—is at last absolved of us. Except,
we notice, someone has just this morning
shouldered the fallen mulberry tree
from the trail, & someone finished the nameplates
for *oak* & *honeysuckle,* has rendered, one
can see, their intricate arboreal
branch-work with all the gaudy reverence
of an amateur. & aren't we? It was
the French who began this labor. Who came
south with their fur trade, & who carried here
the sextants & compasses & their bug
for the new science, with which, I was taught
in the sixth grade, they lopped & divided
& named & measured & mapped the atlas
of the marvelous world. It must have been
a kind of paradise then, no? Its crows
would eat from your hand. Its hickory trees
bore such fruit, reports say, André Michaux
lived all winter on their plenty. The French
imagined their future—children laughing,

democracy, et cetera. Our trail
turns west & we follow, now, through the sedge
& crusted snow to a bluff beyond which,
we observe, the stubbled fields fall away
toward York & Gettysburg. & we can see
our breath as it pools & vanishes. Deer flee.
From the highest location for miles, Milton
says, Michael discloses to Adam the pageant
of history that will follow him—& it
is glorious, mostly. How the banners
blaze from their turrets. With what refinement
the courtesans attend their farandoles
& coronations. Paintings. Waltzes. Also,
however, in the teeming congeries
of men & animals, influenza
racing like a terror. Diphtheria
lifting its lurid flag, & back of this
the banks of 16th-century Europe turned
loose with their sharpened abstraction. He had,
Michaux, heard often of their savagery. Had
called it that, & been properly appalled
when four Lenape entered a schoolhouse
here—winter, 1764—& peeled
their blades across the skulls of the children
as they practiced their numbers. He would have
wept probably, though for the Lenape
it seemed simply the extravagant end
of an entire history of sicknesses
& terror. & you could understand this,
could you not? When finally the earth—or
this goodly frame, a spot, Milton says—starves
us from its jade riversides it will not
be gentle. We know this. We make our way
back together through the honeysuckle
& alders, our garden's great beasts shifting
in their warrens, the river's ice floes
slipping, like us, out to that fallen world
where, today, we will watch the recordings
of some fabulous ball dropping again
through the old year's last seconds. Its smallness—

that's what gets him. How for Adam the vast
globes rolling in their sky lanes, & comets
& stars & *space incomprehensible*
between the moon & Sirius exist
merely—oh, & here he is particularly
brilliant, listen—to *officiate light*
round this dire atom, the world. Round his wife's
hair in its evening coruscations. Her hand
in his hand. & the lush & ample breast
of the new world laid before them. For that,
he thinks, my God, what wouldn't we butcher?

On Iconoclasm; or, A Little History of Statuary Exploding

The true statue can be smashed and yet not die.
    —Wyndham Lewis, *Tarr*, 1914

There exists, he meant, a statue inside
the statue. Something ideal even
the least Platonic of objects, even
the desk lamp's lowered head or next to it
the wine pulsing in its glass imagines
it was made for. That summer what wasn't
indestructible though? England basked. Books
lay out overnight & in the morning
were dry still & their characters returned
to, & still Heathcliff loved Catherine. Sassoon
hunted foxes. The world, the papers wrote
of those months, was most beautiful before
it imploded. Impossible, afterward,
to believe like Lewis some true statue
could endure forever. At Gettysburg
that year the armies—off Water Street, each
in its reunion look—lowered the tarps
& draping from their monuments. Bronze wings
rose from the shoulders of angels. In ranked
stone, solid as faith, great generals swept
their horses about them like cyclones. No
piled stallions. No soldiers cradling their guts
in their hands, homesteads burned, the sycamore
spitting its volley of shrapnel. Perhaps
it is precisely such destruction one
requires statuary after. Imagine,
for instance, some scorched future we finish
expunging each other in—isn't it
something, those enormous Buddhas brooding
on just themselves? No one to watch them. No
one to watch the light at Stonehenge measure—
oh, & what did the living call it?—time
as it moved across the slabs' planes. Today,

on television, some men with sledgehammers
are crushing into a thousand fragments
the Assyrian tablets our alphabets
began on. They are lifting their drills
to the winged, half-human bulls we believed
were divine once. & when they have finished
this work, & when, at last, they have gathered
the scattered westerners left there, & we,
in retribution, & because we are
like them a simple people & vengeful,
have leveled their desert hovels, I hope
there is stirring in the rubble some soul-
like shimmering the whole human species
did not deserve. Undroneable spirit. Dear
reader, there are cultures I have heard of
who will carve for their statues a statue
just like it but smaller—an offering,
they say, in thanks for the stone's surrender
to form. For form read chisels. For chisels,
sweet reader, imagine the instruments
for scoring & hacking we practice with.

Great White

Like the day-moon it is with us

in Mattapoisett. Unveils, for us, always

the same honed fin, fantail, the plane

of the sea sliced open, so that

a part, merely, of the dire beast

suggests the whole. & haven't I

filed my teeth for destruction? Do not

the starched cottages, the Cape's quite

fantastic, far-spreading, salt-knotted

old pines partake, too, of some rank

& bone-rooted Puritan menace? Gem

beaches of Hyannis. Henry James

couchant in Mashpee—"the present

may elbow, yet not jostle the past." As,

indeed, one might recognize walking

the beachfront in Wellfleet—the flags

having held all summer their strict angle

of propriety, the bright bleed-out kits

a kind of power perfected. Every nation

requires its own liege brute by which

to define itself. Exquisite, the incisors

ranked one behind the next, as neat

as 19th-century soldiers. Straight

killer. Clan hunter. What, pray tell,

did you want to hear—that the thing is

nearly extinct? It senses your heartbeat.

&

  Or infinity almost, turned upright. As in
"to sweep & dust & arrange a room

nicely, to wash & iron fine clothes, to cook cakes
    & custards & jellies & cut out & make

    quite a variety of habiliment," mistress
Tryphena Fox enjoined of her slave girl, Maria. Or "e"

& "t" tightened to a cincture. Calligraphic bow. So signifying
    union, perhaps, or contraction. As in Adam

    & his affianced at the field's edge, the angel
above them—swept plumage, flaming sword—for all the world

like some hovering monument. Man
    & woman, thenceforth. Or North

    & South, "our sovereignties & feudal arrangements
are leveled to the ground," one Carolina planter

wept of his spoiled pleasure-tract. Who fashioned
    from the rite & manner of the past their protocol

    of empire. Épées & flintlocks at ten paces. The ladies
poised like mastiffs in the drawing room. Decorum

& dominance. The body
    on horseback, for instance—at Manassas

    & Gettysburg, at Charlottesville, of Lee
& Beauregard—reflects

in its bronze ease the utter authority
    of bloodline, the fine, affected rhetoric

so homesick it seems almost
Eden, antebellum Virginia. Mississippi. You remember

the metaphor, yes? The president, March 1861—"a wife & husband
    may pass beyond the reach of one another, but the different parts

    of a country cannot." Or nation
as doomed beloveds, say— Shut up

in fevered scriptoria, tenth-century monks
    married one letter to the next

    in their painstaking crib-work, one's speed
& economy being for them the exactest augury

of righteousness. Described the coiled glyph
    as *ligature*. As in

    "to bind or fasten." "To flirt." From the hipbone's
bondage & pliancy. The premise—everything

attaches. The twelve-year-old—Ohio, orange tip
    missing from the airsoft replica—lead-

    mangled in his playground gazebo leads south sooner
or later, we know, to the seized runaway bucked

& gagged in the courtyard dust. Instructed
    to sit, a slave drew his knees to his chest then, the leg

    of a table placed beneath his kneecaps, wrists
wrapped around shinbones, bit down

on the overseer's choke-rag. As in—&. Or
    bind rune. Relic insignia. Sigil. Or consider

    a competing account: how, healed
of their motley afflictions—of impotence

often, of gout & pertussis & dog bites—visitants lifted themselves
    like saints from the springs at Gettysburg, emblems,

    the papers reported, "of national deliverance
& regeneration." & praise

Jesus. What people
    is not the undying aspiration of juncture? To one—

    astrological imprint. Another—
a rope wound over itself like a lasso, like

a knot or noose. "Our needles now
    are our weapons," Confederate war bride

    Lucy Butler pencils in her diary
May 24, 1861. Or "ice cream

in summer & oysters in winter" one freedman,
    Owen Robinson, remembered peddling

    for tourists in the war's wake. As in praline
& lemon. As in Malpeques

& Flats & Kumamotos. Bluepoints. Olympias
    & Beausoleils. The tin tray

    sweating with its bounty. The bed of ice—Owen
having crushed it by hand, having

shucked the hinged things himself—
    like diamonds.

BEACH PARTY STEAK FRY

Which Washington, no doubt, dreamt for us
that winter at Valley Forge. & for which,
before this, Revere hung his one lantern
then a second in the Boston belfry, his men
close with their stallions, town shuttered, so when
in the course of human events—or when,
next Sunday, the Kiwanis Club (Upper
Susquehanna Valley branch) bend to their gins
& sodas, or to their rum, umbrella-
festooned cocktails, they will, we know, do so
sipping our finest of freedoms. For us
in America there is little pleasure better
now than this—to feast of our cattle's hind
parts, fried for us, & to let ourselves sink
deep in the combed acre of sand shipped in
to the city park, the Pepsis & Buds
icing in their coolers, couples, for just
ten dollars, drifting against each other
to Joe Vance & the Last Straws, all of which
& more, America, the flier in Sheetz—BEACH
PARTY STEAK FRY—promises. Potato
salad. Ice sculptures. Mojitos. It was
madeira, sixty bottles, Washington
ordered for his friends their final evening
in Philadelphia. From the bar tab—
tumblers (damaged). Claret. Relishes. Men
who it is right, these days, to point out owned
other men & who slaughtered the natives
here but who also, perhaps, allowed us
to forget this sometimes, & to forget,
for once, the Wing Stripz Sheetz's night shift
is frying for me—& which I will relish
now amid the fumes of fueling pickups
with Fanta & Boom-Boom Sauce—are so good,
we know, precisely because they will kill us.

Snow in Inuit

Here we find one word, *aput,* expressing SNOW ON THE GROUND;
another, *qana,* FALLING SNOW; a third, *piqsirpoq,* DRIFTING SNOW . . .
   —Franz Boas, *Handbook of American Indian Languages,* 1911

Poor us, then—winterless. Who want,
still, to believe such surfeit. *Firm pack. Slag
drift.* The myth, I understand, is license
mostly. Boas gone poetic. & yet
imagine that world. Its one snowfall come
into plenty. Its many—one. What whiteness
is not so manifold? So—*squall whip?* If,
I mean, I am the corn fields' flyover-
state vacancies, my neighbors, last year, line-
dancing to Billy Ray Cyrus, the five
Ford Escorts in my father's driveway, I
too am the stitching in the t-shirt—*sic
semper tyrannis*—the medalled veteran
wore as he dropped the truck keys, after, one
then another down a storm drain, April
1995, in Oklahoma. So—*ghost. Sea-
shell. Ivory.* So—in Ohio, on Craigslist, men
lure three strangers to a farm for work
we know now did not exist. For fishing
rights. Sixty dollars per week. One victim
drove from Virginia. It was Christmastime
in the United States. I watched my uncles
deal euchre in the garage, their Busch Lights
sweating in coozies, their conversation
sweet, I remember, as of men—my father
among them—who, in the standard squalor
of their childhood, huddled all winter in
their single hand-sawn bed. What Boas meant
was language is relative. Dependent
on weather & custom. In *thundersnow,*
therefore—in *firn* & *graupel* & *slab,* Scott
Nelson, known then as Scotty Skyfire, falls
again from the Moose Lodge light rigging, his

wrestler's mask crumpled beside him, while I,
six, stare up. In *chop,* syringes of Narcan. Cop
haircuts. Country bars. The Misfit marching
John Wesley to the woods. What part of me
is the six-minute window the white boy
emptied eight magazines in? Which portion
the vertiginous face of the dam the desert
so was humbled by? What *bone & cornsilk—
champagne.* On Baffin, Boas, they say, dragged
his sled three days alone through a blizzard
in fifty below. "The snow terrific." This
meant "dreadful" once, as when—in the age
before I existed—in the pit crew
at Little 500, my father, the jackman,
caught fire near a damaged tank. He tells me
his skin, sometimes, still tingles. Touches
the gleaming slick of forearm. The flames,
he says, were invisible. Isn't that terrific?

Color Guard

... very nearly the spot where the colors stood.
  —monument to 20th Maine, Gettysburg

  Though not—*nearly*
the spot—the spot explicitly, it
  being some question, afterward, where

one man, assigned them, fell then
  another fell, then
one man gathered from the dust

  the colors' standards, the soldiers
forming around him on the hillside, who—moving
  as if on a hinge—swung shut

on the whole hermetic
  & primordial South. Or so
we persuaded ourselves

  in myth. I mean
that only last year—you
  will recall the headlines, how

near the past seemed—the statehouse
  there, & then with the fanfare
of a funeral, let fall

  its blood-stained pennant. Dresses
from a thousand small-town cotillions
  rotted—moth-

et, hems unraveling. I
  could weep, really, for the drawls
of Carolina boys buried

forever now in some back acre
the past is. The flag,
    I can believe, was all of this, though it

was also the bit Bartholomew Davis
    clamped to his slaves' tongues, & was
Percilla, 28, face down

    in the mud & pregnant, her belly
lowered into a hole so as
    the easier to whip her by. When black

residents—Gettysburg, 1863—eyed
    Lee's pickets slipping the passes
they fled fearing just that

    heritage. Others stayed.
They—this
    from witnesses—readied

their homes & there, all month
    we are told, tended both armies'
uncountable wounded. In one room—

    blue. Beside them
Mississippi boys, who believed
    they'd died, or must have, that

gently the residents—ex-
    slaves some of them—swept
the hair from their faces

    & bathed them, that
carefully they piled their limbs. Oh it
    is fitting, surely, the colors

of the South furled out
    nowhere today in our battlefield's
strict choreography. Though Lee

roosts majestic on his stallion. Though Sunday
mornings the color guard marches
    their flag, the Union's, through town

to work again the difficult regimen
    of pomp. Complexly
they wheel, one of the men

    circling his partner, the others,
then, stepping
    neat into the pattern as if

by such care—*very nearly*
    the spot—by such
fine fidelity to guard

    the single history given us
to speak of. Always
    it is present. I remember

halftime from the bleachers—our band's
    flag girls whirling like smoke, their semaphore
flashing. Some relic

    pageantry we are fashioned
of blood & all. Afterward
    the players lumbered, hulking

& terrible, to the field. Floodlights
    trembled. I remember
I wanted to be them.

Local News

Or dearest theater.
                              Aren't we
all, the premise is, for one
                    half hour, in tight zoom, suitable
for history?
            A Lyndhurst couple
married Monday at the tire shop. The suspect
                    who fled the Chevron holdup
on horseback. Athens
        was less its democracy—solemn
                              ecclesia, Draco's
                    torts precedent—than
the price of goat's milk in the Way
                of Sheepherders. Ahead
at five—teens skipping sleep. Teens
            at St. Cecilia's filling the boot
            for Alzheimer's. Behind the co-hosts
the city poses on its screen.
            Sunset flashes.
                        For a minute
our sundry lesser dramas—our bodies
        pulled from retention ponds, holiday
                    toy lineups—form
a single American skyline.
            Small nation
of lotto & weather radar.

                    The ecclesia—they
did so, they believed, to banish
            the idea of distance—prohibited
                star-gazing, so faithful
they were to the vine & polis.

                    At Taco Bell
yesterday, two men

pulled knives on each other because,
they said, of a woman. One
drove off with her. The other
sacked Troy.

Indianapolis 500

If anything in this world is bulletproof, this is it.
    —Joe Cloutier, Indianapolis Motor Speedway president, 1985

Still, they inspect our coolers. Cameras
wheel silent in their bubbles, the bomb dogs
of the heartland tending the aisles. *Bulletproof*
is such strict labor. Today, still, soldiers
wipe the dust from their rifles in a street
in the desert somewhere so I, home here
from Pennsylvania, can crack Natural
Ices open one after another & watch
the million multicolored balloons lift off
from their terraced pagoda, the globes
of blue & red wrapped tight, I imagine,
in tiny flak jackets. From the back seats
of forty convertibles, Chevy, veterans
smile & gesture for the crowd, crisp flags
rising from the grandstands, the pit crews, clean
still in their firesuits, sliding their jet cars
into position. The infield reels. This
is your nation on myth. Remember moon
landings? The pageantry we packed them off
in their fiery candles with. Or think of Rome
late in its decadence. Its legions beat
back in Gaul & Cyprus, though the empire
of course was the stench & glory roiling
on the stadium floor. This Memorial Day
weekend in Washington tourists queue past
our first papers saved there in bulletproof
glass, but the hot dogs dripping on their coils
in the Alley Cafe, gate six, are the Word
made flesh, the fire rippling in the engines
suddenly, flag lifted, & we are one
then in our dying to watch a man, moon-
shot, or like some classic hero, hitch on
the armor of his people—plastic wings
fanned outward, chassis gleaming—& turning
to his distant, deathless gods go airborne.

What Though the Field Be Lost

Thus Satan, perched on the oblivious Pool—
>   prime secessionist, Rebel King. "That were low indeed," he says,
>   "to bow & sue for grace / With suppliant knee."

Hell, around him, throbbing.

>   •

By this time, Milton has fled. Two wives dead, two children in the
>   ground at St. Margaret's, he vanishes for a moment from history.
>   The King, Charles, whom he'd opposed, parades on London. In
>   Smithfield—a false floor. His funeral staged.

>   •

Take Tenney, for one, to his sweetheart in Ohio— "My dear," he calls
>   her, then *"the first secessionist was Satan."*

Or Brownlow, of Knoxville. 1860, the *Whig*— Satan "seceded from a bet-
>   ter Government than our Cotton States did, but from the same
>   motives."

Always, that is, the impulse to likeness. A *kind* of thing, this—

>   •

One tradition—
>   townies, the Fourth, plant plastic flags for Gettysburg's fallen.
>   Flush with the gravestones, they grow, my wife & I pretend, from
>   the mouths of the soldiers beneath us.

We call them that—"fallen."

>   •

When Blake, though, in 1790 names Milton "of the Devil's party," he does not mean politics—God, i.e., as Charles rescendant. He means Milton "was a true Poet," & could we still—satisfied, so, in our righteousness—admire that?

& he *is* charismatic. The gallant, Satan. [*Sighs from the balcony.*]

Notice, in Eden, how he falters before the Deception. "Should I," he asks—an aside, for us—"at your harmless innocence / Melt, as I do . . ."

Dear Satan.

Dear sweet, of the Light & furnace.

•

Of burials here, by accident—eight. The gray of their uniforms, to interment crews, a kind of colorless blue. On belt plates, epaulettes— "VA" mistaken for "PA." &c. The kinship, then—letter-close.

These men we decorate last.

"Taps" plays.

The faith—flag with its crossed bars, "blood-stained"—is not, one should understand, our own. Most, though, were conscripted. Cropped before that an acre or two they paid rent on. *Redneck.* One should understand—

•

So Milton, on Being. Who believes, even as he is hunted, one Substance quickens everything—angel & Fiend, fir trees, the tiered revetments of copper mines.

Seraphim, therefore, flitting through their precincts, feel hunger. Fuck, as we do.

"Whom obstacle"—[*almost winking, Raphael*]—"find none / Of membrane, joynt, or limb."

•

Or "Lucifer," they called him, & often that year—

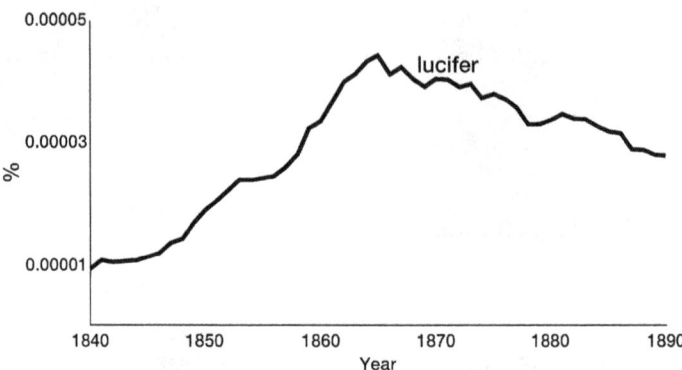

Perhaps, admittedly, the matchbooks—*Lucifers.* Packaged for Union soldiers, Satan prancing on the wrapper, they were—with ironclads, standardized time—the decade's preeminent innovation.

Daylight, at a touch.

•

Duncan, for his part, cites Shakespeare instead—Iago. "The poet's role," he writes—1971, to Levertov—"is not to oppose evil, but to imagine it."

Imagine that, in 1971.

•

On earth, the angels merely sigh.

Slumped on their Northern monuments, they watch the ghost tours moving like cattle. Cast-bronze, Honor gawks skyward.

•

Of splendor, though—the Southerners lunging toward death. The rifle
     one man—Mississippi, the sculptor De Lue—uses, butt-end, to
     defend the colors as they waver.

One man, his brother, bracing the flags. Face, with its rictus.

•

We see, we say, how they could do it—

Natinals

Company apologizes for Washington Nationals jersey error
    —ESPN.com, April 23, 2009

By then, we'd seen our mistake.

A nation

was what really—words,

some stitchwork? & if

just one letter were missing—slipped,

maybe, to the sweatshop floor,

or forgotten

that week in a pattern book

in Matamoros

over lunch break—what,

then, of our bomber crews

waiting at Ramstein? What

of our electoral system

& glocks & Preamble? For three

& two-thirds innings, not one of us

noticed. The sodium lights

blazed on the field's green canton, catcher

& pitcher passing their slender line

between them, efficient

as a sewing machine.

So the flaw

would come to define us. Like

a snagged thread. Yes,

like the run

in the hem of the loincloth Achilles

wore, or one

of those other ancient oxes too proud

or dumb for their own survival.

Script itself
came earlier. In Egypt,
            in turquoise shafts, slave families
        scored prayers in the dazzling walls.
                        This was, we
largely accept, the origin
            of America. O,

            my doomed country. One day
we too will surface
        with our stadiums. Faded white
                domes & mezzanines. Excavators
will marvel at our box scores'
        strict cuneiform, the crude
                    acrostics—FOX,
        TBS—the men of this nation
        raised to their one god.

                I want them
to remember us smiling. The diamond's
            brown lanes raked clean, our cups
        sloshing with the flattest of beers. Some boys,
they will say, chase a ball
                around a field to no end
            save beauty.

                But I know
this isn't us. Our custom
        is ancient & terrible. There
            is a hero who is all of us, one
                nation on his chest—cloud-
gatherer, breaker
            of horses. He parades
        dreadfully, behold, to the plate.

Gapers Delay; or, Mise en Abyme with Fire & Corsage

If we shadows have offended,
Think but this, and all is mended,
That you have but slumber'd here
While these visions did appear.
    —Puck, *A Midsummer Night's Dream*

Or think the roadside inferno folding
back into itself. Think, instead—as each
of the fairy kingdom's capers resolves,
finally, into dancing—the family
gathered through their windshield, scattered
bits of sheet metal & glass collapsing
behind them into form. It is one thing,
of course, in the charmed midsummer forest
art is. Another, perhaps, imagining
the traffic report this morning—Montrose
jammed to the bridge, inbound Eisenhower
three lanes of wreckage—rewinding itself
to weather. While I am brushing my teeth
a landscaping trailer, the radio
says, has jackknifed on Roosevelt, & south
traffic, rapt, watches as it slows & it
is almost, they think, a sort of painting
they are seeing, bright lawnmowers thrown off
like flowers in their airborne arrangements
of blades. Rakes fluttering. Rubbernecking
it is known as elsewhere. Or spectator
traffic. Gawk block. Gape train. In Ohio
the Friday of our senior Prom, we watched
the paramedics collect MacKenzie Flessner
from some hacked-up Corolla towed there
for precisely that purpose. We believed it
all for a moment. They lowered her neck
in the stretcher's collar. They carried her
around the block in their ambulance. All art,
the point is, aspires likewise to wrench us

from complacency. To make us
turn, suddenly, toward some spectacular mess
made pleasing, Puck understands, exactly
as it fails to involve us. It is Puck,
after all, who explains at play's end every
sword brandished in the rude mechanicals'
one-act masque is fake—made, he says, by Snug
joiner, & Flute the bellows mender. The men
in that play take their names, you will observe,
as we used to, from their labor. Starveling
the tailor. Tinker. Smith. It was my father's
business literally, once, to wreck
cars against a concrete wall, & to note
in the cameras' still lives the precise
angles a Cadillac crumpled at, or how,
to the millisecond, a Chevy's side-
impact airbags burst, though not one hour
of that work—wrecker, mangler of steel—stopped
the eighteen-wheeler one night, late, from taking
our Ford against its grille a quarter mile
down Interstate 70. Everything
slowed. Glass popped. We caromed across
its trailer, & if I inform you—oh
my curious, slack-jawed groundling—how, or
the hundred ways we should have died that night
will you picture, as I do still, its sets
of smoking wheels buckling the A-pillar
inches from my father's head? Oh will you,
my gape-monger, imagine the traffic
westbound? Those expensive, delicate cars
that must have seen something dazzling, a man
& boy swept up in their calamitous
slow dance of blood & plastic. Gasoline
blooming. We are having an accident
I said to my father, whose name, Kempf, meant
"fighter" once, or "warrior." Remember
this began in the forest. In the gym's
rafters, little cutout fairies folded
their wings. The bunting & streamers our trees
were made from fluttered in the evening's

pink breeze. & when it was over, the ice
melting in its punch bowls, the last sad song
gone quiet, we walked to our cars—MacKenzie
Flessner who lived, & Tim Stewart & Steph
Montgomery & I, & Jesus & Shakespeare
& a bottle of Boone's Farm my father
had bought for us just this once—we went out
into the darkness & started its engine.

The Union Forever

The field lay all before us. That first
evening we could almost see
        the South's skirmish lines furling out
like a ribbon. Pickett
    whirling on his stallion.
                On Cemetery Ridge
Union monuments threw their shadows
            across the breastworks.
                 That first evening
the light lured itself
      west down the faces of Pennsylvania's
            low bluffs, beyond which
   California, so late
           our home, turned to gold
without us—its nothing
         history, groves
    of concrete & sex.
             Our Penske truck
idled near the Angle. The engine
         ticked til it cooled.

   •

"This area is the most thoroughly improved I ever saw.
Apples, quinces, &c. in utmost profusion, and bee hives
ad infinitum. Wheat, corn, half a dozen varieties of grass
met the eye at every turn, all in rock or strong and closely
built wooden fences."
  —Pvt. John C. West, 4th Texas, June 1863

   •

At which, the fence-rows,
        the Rebel army, advancing
      here on its copse of trees, stopped
to open its passage.
      Anatomy

of single-family livestock farming.
                                        Our free state's
mute resistance, therefore, to the sweep
        & pomp of plantation slavery. To acre
                                cotton, swamp Louisiana's
rice paddies. To Master
        gazing from his window. *Amen,*
                        the very stones would cry out.

                •

        In Gettysburg
                        it was summertime.
                                We tilled the side yard—year
of our engagement—
                        for sweet corn. We sat out
        all season in our swimsuits, in
                                love, in lawn
                chairs with fruit & cocktails. Corey
read Whitman. We knew,
                I suppose, that soldiers—
        day one—had fallen gut-shot
                        in our driveway. We found it
simple to forget this. In so
        charming a place to forget—Whitman,
                        1863—*the heap*
                        of feet & arms, et cetera. Men
sawed into stumps. Men cut
                        away from themselves—it was
        not lost, the simile—like
                the nation they had risen for.
                                Our fruit
                shone in its dishes. In swim masks
neighbor kids filled their guns
        at our garage's spigot.

                •

        What though
                        would be a just form

38

of remembrance? It was a year
    of champagne & police shootings. Statues
                      toppled. Schoolkids
      tracked Pokémon across the hill—the high-
water mark, men named it—
        where Armistead, saber flickering
    above him like lens-flare, fell
               from his horse
   into eternity. Where, wavering
  momentarily—the music
             swelling, slow pan
     across the ridgeline—the South lapped back
on itself like a flood. For months
      I dreamed of storm surge.
               In the morning
Segway tours moved
  in silhouette against the statues. In slash
      marks. Imagine—
              everywhere
  the line breaking.

  •

WHO GAVE UP THEIR LIVES IN DEFENSE OF A PERPETUAL
UNION WHO FELL UPON THIS FIELD WHO ELSEWHERE
DIED UNDER THE FLAG THIS MONUMENT IS DEDICATED

  •

       As for us,
we strutted like models. Bronze
  in our suntans, young
      still, we arranged ourselves
in the season's poses. The Peach
     Orchard, day two—we kissy-
  faced for the camera above us.
      Beyond the lens
    the sky of Pennsylvania laid out
  as it had, once, for soldiers
       as they rested. Shellfire

sailed above them in parabolas.
                              Who lacked the words
                    flight path. Who lacked
          vector & *arc.* "I watched a dark
                    line flit overhead," one said. One said,
          "lines toward every angle
                              of the compass." So some kind
of marvelous poetry pulled its contrail
          across the firmament.
                              The photographs
one is likely familiar with—one
                              of these men face up
     in a tangle of rocks, a rifle
                    propped beside him—were staged,
          we know, for ideal effect.
                              My favorite—
we are romping together toward sunset.
                              Reckless.
                              We understand
nothing, yet, of the endless ways
                    we will hurt each other, in awe
          still of our own
                    dumb beauty. Nobody
          is saying we have not suffered. They are just
such civilized photos.

          •

     From Round Top,
                    the guidebooks note, the fields fall off
in terraces. There
          is goldenrod & ginger.
                              Beebalm. *Dicentra*
     eximia—bleeding heart. There are
                    cooper's hawks & wood thrushes. One
could have a picnic
          really, though we
          savored in our car our McDonald's
     fries & milkshakes. A Coke. *So,*
                    we said, *American.*

                            All war,
gapers came with their finery.
                  Field glasses. Baskets
    of port & fougasse. Congressmen
  hired carriages afterward
                     & rode out—oak
coolers filled with champagne, the prostitutes
        dazzling in their hoop skirts—to see
  for themselves the rumored field.
                   They found
their country. Love,
                I will watch with you
til we are broomsedge. The asters
  opening ther mouths
              in the Slaughter Pen. We fed
each other fats in manifold forms.
           Starlings lifted. This place,
  we said, for the life of us—

    •

ON THIS GROUND FOR THEIR RIGHTEOUS CAUSE IN
GLORY THEY SLEEP WHO GAVE TO IT THEIR LIVES TO VALOR

    •

            But first
      they buried the corpses. Before
the monuments' bronze rhetoric, black troops
    paced the field with their shovels.
                They sang
folk hymns, hung garlic
     around their necks, so wretched
      & swollen were the bodies. Blowflies
laid eggs in the corpses' nostrils.
          John Moffett,
  alive still, his skull shot away
        above the temple, touched his brain
as it flaked into coral petals.
         Remember, rarely

were there coffins. They covered them
                              in knapsacks, the shirts,
                    sometimes, off their backs. That gently
they kept them from the dirt.
                                        It was the work
            of one man to make them
gravestones. They
                        christened him Letterer.

                •

"Deep, boys, deep—so the beasts won't get me."
    —Pvt. Jeremiah Gage, 11th Mississippi, July 1863

                •

            The past, that year, kept coming back
like a fever. In College Park,
                at a bus stop, a supremacist . . .
            In Stamford, on a garage door . . .
                                    Everywhere
white men carried torches.
                        Mornings were hammered pewter.
                        Starless.
                                    I ran repeat
        miles down West Confederate, fell,
        I admit, in love
                        a little with the statues' sense
of nostalgia. Their syntax
                like a burning cross.
                            Would we not,
                    though—living then, as they
        did, in Vicksburg,
                        say, in brocaded
        evening skirts, a suit
            merely for fox hunting—have made Mississippi
our god?
                    Election night,
                            I heard howling
        & whooping from the Mine Saloon.

                              "You understand,"
David said—a student, a
                    black man—"most days
          we want to kill all of you."

          •

                    & one morning, dawn—a Silverado
on Cemetery Ridge. In its bed, erect
          on a home-built dais, a Confederate flag
                    rippling like a bedsheet. For an hour
he cruised the breastworks, as if,
     we thought, to embody
                    there some last-ditch ghost dance. Dead
South. *Tourist*,
          we called him,
                              & ran.

          •

WE SLEEP HERE IN OBEDIENCE TO LAW WHEN DUTY
CALLED WE CAME WHEN COUNTRY CALLED WE DIED

          •

     The Fourth, though, we floated
gauzily among rattan tables.
                         Cicadas buzzed.
                    Some country
ballad drifted from an iPhone, above
                    all of which Douglass—*what
to the slave
          is the Fourth of July*—listened,
                    once, to a people's plainsong
                    rising like bier-smoke. We saw
from our lawnchairs only
     the fireworks wilting in their spheres, a show
                    of light & color which was
for us the echo
          always of some prior artillery.

                                            Consider
Pickett waiting in the treeline. The two-
                        shot signal. The skirt of lead
        his army lowered before him, single
    loudest sound yet heard
                            on the continent. Consider
Douglass, 1852—what,
                        to the slave,
            is your Preamble? Your paper
        lanterns dangling in their trees—

            •

"An eagle in the very midst of the thunderstorm might
have experienced such confusion. Milton's account of the
great battle between the forces of good and evil, which
originated in this same question of secession, gives some
faint idea of this artillery duel."
    —Pvt. John C. West, 4th Texas, July 27, 1863

            •

        So it was, for them,
                    a question—secession. So that
    when Davis rose in the Senate, when spy balloons
                lifted from the Rappahannock, the hard
    scholars in Cambridge
                debated synecdoche. Gk.—
                                    the understanding one
            with the other. Just what,
        they asked, is a country.
                            The conscripted,
        that night, fitted their stories into history—part
for the whole. Most
                owned no slaves. Most surgeons
        cut quickly.

            •

            Why not, then, ten flavors

   of cupcake? Guests
           from California. Torches. Why not
                  the pinwheel centerpieces? My
war-bride. My white-
             organza'd. Who,
  long runs—the sunlight
                 a kind of breathing
     in the mist, the low hills
   shrouded—would stop
          near Culp's field to pet the calves,
                    just risen. For that
men shouldered to the wall. Who called it
  love, then. One
            & one. Brother,
        sometimes, against brother. Thus
civil. Syn.—
       gracious, complaisant. Sweet,
                  like a country
     we wed.

   •

"The men are in splendid spirits. The smell of the dead is
awful. We have all got sixty-five crackers to celebrate the
day with."
  —Samuel Russel, 96th Pennsylvania, July 12, 1863

   •

  & when the day came, the rain
                  came with it. We swept
our clutch of well-wishers—fetched,
            that is, our mothers, some
          champagne flutes—to a room
  where men, we knew, let part of their bodies go
to preserve their bodies. Not
         whole, precisely. Her white was
  eggshell. Antique.
              Bone. There would be
a fact here. That surgeons,

called "operators," knotted the veins
  & arteries of their patients
                            with horsehair. That here,
on the Fourth of July, Lee's army
               reeled south in just such
  a Pennsylvania rainstorm. In lace
                   finery, in archival
         ink we authored our names. I take you
Corey, I said, til death do
              us part.

       •

PERFORMING THEIR SACRED DUTY AS THEY UNDER-
STOOD IT THEIR NAMES ARE INSCRIBED ON FAMES
IMMORTAL SCROLL

       •

  & so we drove south. In summer fever,
        at sunrise. A rented Mustang. *Just*
  Married on the rear windshield.
                      We understood this
as pilgrimage, part
      of our people's dear ritual. In the distance,
the steeples of Charleston threaded the fog—called
        "Holy," the city
               like a glassed relic. Sumter
lay flat & irredeemable in the harbor.
                 How pleasing
      we found it to wander—whole
        South like a bathhouse—from heat
  to air-conditioning. Oysters
              terraced on ice. I took this
from Charleston—when Sumter fell,
  Confederate gunners removed their hats. History
        is like that,
            there.

       •

It was, we admitted though,
                    the South's statuary—West
Confederate, Pennsylvania,
            the 21st century—
                              we most admired. Art
as compensation, grace, spring rainstorms
                sweeping the delta.
                              In De Lue's
        Louisiana monument, Saint Barbara—of
    armorers & firemen,
                    artillery—lifts,
            true to her patronage, a flaming
        mortar shell in her upturned palm. Plays
in the other the trumpet—
                        fluted, gold—
    of resurrection, the dead man
                    at her feet a gunner
        in New Orleans's artillery.

                        Shoelaces ragged. Imagine
how desperately they believed. Before
                    we raze the thing, place
        your hand in the gunner's palm.
    It is open, oversized
                    like his feet, the sculptor's
trademark.
            You can touch it.

        •

    But mainly, I miss the cows.
                        On Culp's Hill,
evenings, you can see them
            feeding in their pasture. The shadows
    will lengthen, some last
                pressed thinness of light laying itself
on the switchgrass. The calves,
                    just born,
            will wobble behind you. For them,
the grass—the golden

wave rising in its distances, Whitman's
      hair of graves—that grass
             is only the grass. Good
cows—I could love us
      that faithfully. They are,
           sometimes, so close
you can hear them breathing

•

"The time may vary a few months, or even a few decades, but the job will be settled and that all right too. I am, in this matter, like St. Paul's Charity, ready to bear, believe, hope, and endure all things for the cause, knowing if we do, we also, like Charity, shall never fail. This has been a most egotistical letter."
   —William Wheeler, 13th New York, July 26, 1863

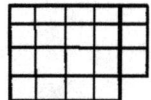

Homecoming

Gettysburg Area High School

 Here though a faith
the nation could be salvaged with—
                                  pick & roll
        drills at pregame, layup lines. Here skyhooks
   hanging like ornaments.
                                    In America
our monarchs sit courtside, queen
                             shining in her cheap tiara,
        texting, the men
   of the king's cortege letting Milk Duds
                    arc cleanly to each other's mouths. How
coolly they reign, as if
        at last, after history, this were
                              in fact our home. Here
ghost tours & pup tents.
                    Cycloramas. Here bronze artillerists
                        studding the tended lanes
   of our battlefields.

        For irony—after
                          the amputations, after
the lice & gut rot, the war
                came home, at Appomattox,
    to a living room. Here Lee
            slack in a caned loveseat. With company
            in the anteroom,
                        Edmund Ruffin, wrapped
in Confederate flags, fitting a rifle
    to his mouth
                for forever. Isn't there

                always, afterward, a touch
    of domesticity? A marriage feast,
                        Luke calls heaven, a home
of many dwelling places.

Perfumes. Sun decks.

Of redemption,
though, I know
no finer form
than the wheel route the Warriors' star freshman
runs from the free-throw line,
the forward cutting, guard
passing to a spot the stretch four
has not yet arrived at.

Here emancipated
slave families lifting the roof beams
of the future. Couldn't you
believe that history
were a husk merely?

Here,
in the small country of the gym, jump shots
rain like mercy. Men
press their bodies together, the pep band's
saxes glittering, our queen

with her retinue bending,
now, to accept their sashes.

Afterward
there will be dancing. Bounce houses. Here,
the chips & bunting. The ball
made of plastic scattering one light
in a thousand directions at once.

Cyclorama

Only with such care could history
take form. For years
    workers scraped rotted acrylic

from the canvas. Accretions
    of bug frass. For years
they in-painted the fields & generals then,

    with surgical instruments, sewed in
a fiberglass corset, hung the thing
    like a gown so we

can admire from a platform the order
    in Pickett's death parade. Neat
lines marching in echelon. Perspective

    like a minor god's. We have come,
like tourists, to believe this. That we,
    from a certain angle, made clean

in the workers' emulsions, are one
    in our manicured history. We could be
at the beach. We

    could be at the Blue & Gray getting tight
on three-dollar margaritas, "Tequila Sunrise"
    playing on the TouchTunes, the usual

locals beginning to sway. So we are
    obedient citizens today. We lean out
above the guns & wagons the workers

    have added around the platform, fake
horsepaths winding off
    toward the hem of the painting. *Impossible,*

a Boston newspaper reported
    at the unveiling, *to say*
where the illusion begins. A veteran—

    I will show you where I stood.
You see this
    was before the Internet. No satellite

or drone lowered its camera
    yet to the field's frenzy. When men marched
back to their campsites, they could know,

    of battle, barely more
than the curtain of musket smoke
    they had moved inside, the smell

of the man beside them. There,
    though, around the bonfire
of their grief, they pieced their stories

    together into narrative. This one,
he swears, saw a pair
    of Union lieutenants torn clean

from their horses by grapeshot. Someone
    watched the ghost of Stonewall Jackson
weeping near the Peach Orchard. Just so,

    the docent tells us, the workers
stitched the painting's eighteen panels
    together to a landscape. Size

of a football field. A flag
    they named like a tilt-a-whirl. What more
could we honor ourselves so rightly

    with? We exit
through the entrance. To mend it
    completely they sewed back the sky.

Nativity Scene Dedication

All the new carols are godless. Although
the children do their best—bright faces flushed
with songs about yule bears, with blue Christmas
cacti waiting for snow. Of salvation—
we take, these days, what comes. Kiwanis men
serve hot dogs from their car trunks. Road flares
blaze. Woodsmoke. Lo, in the darkness, in carved
maple, in the lot of the AutoZone, oxen
fall to their knees for the Christ child. Tonight,
he is bestial again in his trough. Doll-
plump. Mongrel. All summer the restorers
chiseled & planed. Laid doves in newsprint. This,
that a people—scared mostly, or alone
here on its bough of the Milky Way—might
for once remember its goodness. If grace,
I mean, is not the lacquered shepherds star-
eyed with their livestock—is not, behold, the line
of sports fans filing from Chuck's Bar, who bring
presently unto the Lord their orders
of cheese fries, myrrh, the stable fetid, foals
dropping their necks like oil pumps—what then
is the shape of deliverance? In the window
of the AutoZone, chrome DeSotos turn
in their tiered display. Spray waxes gleam. *Go,*
a voice says. A star above us unspools
its curtain of light. Christ slumbers. The sky
at dawn, they say on Earth, is the reflection
of trapped combustion gasses. If it is that,
in the end, we are to pray toward—let us pray.

Little America

Before the snack bar—before
        the pools & Wi-Fi & truck scales—the place
is covenant merely.
                For two states
        billboards herald its plenty—bedspreads
starched white as bridal gowns, goose-down
                pillowcases.
                        Steak fries.

                                Why
wouldn't, in Europe, the pure products
        of Luther level their compasses
to this? Its lush acreage. Its
        Coors & fueling islands a kind
    of continent in miniature—little
                New World. Or what
are all the lopped Venuses
                in Paris, the paintings
   of fruit & kings & annunciations against
        these taxidermied beauties?
                    Bright cases
packed with squirrel & muskox.
                Ain't that
             America? Where
      the AC whirrs. Where
   the best pecan pie west
      of Peoria is served,
            still, on beveled Tiffany. Isn't
we all aristocrats?

            Only,
     of history—in
   a lot near the Welcome Center, size
            of the pinyon trees—a green
       fiberglass dinosaur remains. The money
is oil, it means. We gorge
   here on the bit

       & dispersants. Land rights.
                    Pipe fracture. Though

the hot tubs remain spotless—nozzles
   like finned turbines,
                     bronze fixtures. Give them
your poor & your wretched. Give them
              your travelers—tempest-
   wracked, white-
knuckled, your blacked-
     out & bloodshot, dodgers
                  of trucks & RVs. All this
in our roadside democracy.
   Free air. 80-cent
      swirl cones. Home,
                writ small,
       as stitchwork.

The Fishhook

As in the barbed contour the Union line—last ramparts til Washington—resembled.

South like a snagged muskie, therefore.

"A grunting weight," writes Bishop, "battered & venerable."

•

This is an ancient story—how a doomed, extravagant ideal dies. A line of troops turned back on itself & sharpened.

•

Perched behind his gelding, our guide stares into the shimmering distances. To him, it is not quite, of course, the past. "A third brigade falls back presently from our left," he tells us. "Stonewall is gone."

It is early in our marriage.

•

What Lee had imagined were hammer strikes, successive death-blows— "one body," the guide informs us, "exactly coordinated."

•

Canonical, the body he imagined.

Before the war, on a thousand small-town Southern plantations, plaster kouroi swept back their shoulders in defiance. A plantation, that is, being no respectable empire without one.

Apollo in strict proportion—the fine chessboard of the obliques.

Or imagine the plumb line from sternal crest to navel. *Linea alba.* Translation— "white line."

　　　•

What are we if not fearfully fashioned?

　　　•

The two teenagers, though—supreme in their abandon, bodies like a heart muscle—fucking beneath Brigadier General John Geary need hardly bother with history.

Horse-hauled, Corey & I, old enough already to sigh for their ardor, sweat.

We sway against each other in love with our own lost past—that sentimental. Six times per day in Charleston. In Miami, the midnights febrile & lush.

Our horse drops hay-studded nuggets.

　　　•

The flaw, our guide explains—"acoustic shadows."

So that, though McLaws's cannons echo as far as Harrisburg, Ewell, two miles away, hears nothing. Waits three hours for the two-shot signal.

One body, synchronized with itself or not.

　　　•

This is an ancient story. The South hoisted to the sunlight—seizing.

　　　•

This is an ancient story—the past comes back. Believe that.

In 1875, the White Line levels its rifles on a crowd of black men in Vicksburg. '76 Association. Pale Faces. Knights of the White Camellia. Klan.

Or Bishop again—"infested."

•

But consider George Warner, artillerist in the 20th Connecticut.

When his Napoleon explodes, our home not far, he watches both arms ripped from their sockets.

His shoulders gape.

You understand—this meant the end of it.

•

Who, twenty years later—the pulleys rigged, rope knotted around his waist like a war medal—walks backward to unveil his monument.

In bronze—"who marched with Sherman to the sea."

In the photograph afterward, his wife holds a cannonball & his baby.

•

This place, named for a fishing implement.

•

Listen—we work with the weapons left us.

Pro Patria

For that they loaded their rifles. For that,
air thick with metal, they stepped to the wall
& rose, & the glory on them then—men,
you understand, who signed their names, no, not
for money this war, or for land—laid down,
their stone says, a most magnificent fire.
Galling fire. Withering fire. A fire fine
& pleasing it was to the Lord. Like grain
threshed, the enemy—et cetera. Summer
in Pennsylvania. All month the buses
with their tourists glide back & forth, fishlike,
down Confederate Avenue. They pass
slowly in their Jeeps & Escalades, great
gallant Northern generals flickering
off their windshields, the South's small plaques
flashing once in the light then darkening.
History, no doubt, is like that. Imagine,
for instance, the long line of Virginians
rippling the near slope. Who saw, or must have,
almost, beyond the Union cannon, lamp light
shimmering in New York City. Or saw,
stretched before them like a field, that future
they had risen for. Flood plain. Plain of fruit
& majesty. & lavish, I would say. See
how the park's yellow-vested lawn crews prune
& arrange their landscape—"manicurists"
they are called—so not one wheat blade ripens
that was not here. How, when the birds returned
& the armies, exhausted, wandered back
to their borders, the bureaucracies—complex
& vast—attending them swept the field. They
tallied their dead. It is not staggering.
Seven, a stone says. Three flags. A horse. Here
for the final time a word was equal,
then, to our grandeur & fury. It was
with splendid appearance with colors raised
in glory & just was their cause & just

was their sacred & valor. & for that,
we know, they wrote to their children. For that
they picked their way, wheeling now & stepping
light among their marvelous dead. Not yet,
for them, that keen-edged irony Owen
sharpened in York & Picardy, & which,
you will note, our poem today mainly
refuses. But I want to tell you now
that across the Bloody Angle busloads
of students with fidget-spinners slam Dews
at the town's newest McDonald's. I want
to tell you that these summers the cities
of America are filled with the bodies
of young black men though for that, I have read,
the country collapsed once & split. No—
dulce the monuments say, which is sweet
in American. & it is. Tonight
here, the cows in their pastures, fat for us
& who sag with their plenty, will let down
their heads in a beautiful country. & I,
who have not suffered, will sit in a bar
they call the Blue & Gray & will drink beer
with the bikers & college kids, our gins
& sodas, our pitchers of Rolling Rock
sweating in their glasses, & there will be
sweet music on the jukebox & all of us
will swear to you, yes, we will tell ourselves
it is beautiful. It is beautiful.

Good Death

ars moriendi

                All season they've practiced. In back
of the Visitors Center, in dress
                      regalia—gray
                fatigue blouses, blue wools
             trimmed with shoulder cord—they
have tumbled faultlessly
    through their thousand forms
                    of departure. The artful
                gut-shot. Clutchers
          at shinbones. Whimperers. One man,
I've learned, drives from Elmira merely
    to fall first for his comrades.
                      Like Christ,

  we'd have said once, who left
                  behind him a kind
      of ideal passing—his ecstatic
pep talk, the acceptance—our 19th century
                so admired they made it
fashion. Practiced,
    Sundays, the faces their final moments
         would be sealed with.

           When Amos Humiston—
wounded, witnesses say, day one
    on Stratton Street—collapsed
            into heaven, he stared to the end
at portraits of his children in tintype. Little
            Frederick. Alice,
                  in a dress
of the same stock burlap the workbench
    behind her wears.

        This was—recall
in Thackeray, Dickens—the Victorian

                              death scene, sentimental
as Amos could manage it. His family—
    in miniature, in imagination
                          strictly—considering
                    each sigh & cheek twitch
for redemption. & let us

                    go so deliberately—
    good death, the readiness
                          to walk, with light
            blazing around us like a bonfire, across
the border to Elysium.
                          Wheat fields. Seraphim.
                                As if

            they could master it, the men
    jerk through their last contortions. They tear
at imitation buttons, B-movie
                    their way to the shade trees. They
are so good
            at death—face down
                    in the past, in the afterlives,
                          finally, of soldiers
they almost are. In the cave

    Christ panics first,
                          just for a second. Then
he remembers.

"South Will Rise"

Once in a K-Mart bathroom, Dayton. One
time, driving, the roof of a corn silo
west of Muncie. Upstairs tonight—the town
my home this year, the bar themed—a phoenix
in black Sharpie sending itself into flight
on the woodgrain. The phrase—blade-cut. Late
September in Gettysburg—our tourists
thinned to day-trippers, the first football games
of the season on surround. I drink Yuengling
& watch Samantha, our bartender, garnish
two glossy manhattans with the spiral
of a lemon rind. He meant, I think, the man
who wrote this—in Michigan, a billboard
spray painted, a barn in Racine once—not
swept porches in the shade of magnolias, not
malt shops or Dale Earnhardt, pitchers of tea
thick with sugar, though still I have not asked
the strict Southerners who come here—Harleys
sailing their banners behind them, Chevy
Silverados caked with window stickers—if,
for them, the bronze statues on Baltimore
mark too the end of Skoal & cotillion, long
drawl, crawdaddies, the spit can. Is it not,
I mean, a manner of pilgrimage? Maybe
weeping sometimes for Louisiana they see
spread before them black men moving again
in the fields of Pennsylvania. Maybe
they watch some long ribbon of gray gather
itself & rise. Look—isn't all myth this
faithful? A savior, Christ for instance, slipped
under & three days later the cave mouth
shining. Dionysus ripped to fretwork
then whole. *I am who . . .* Haven't we
always, sad little death-species, understood
ourselves part somehow of the gods' going
below—always like it is nothing—only
to return? When Persephone, indentured

to hell's slow shade-meadows, lowers herself
back through the cleft earth—to Hades, to her
jeweled grenade—we too, the living, lay in
together our own lean harvest. Fort Wayne
once, in back of a Chipotle. On Steinwehr
this weekend, beyond the t-shirt vendors
& ghost tours, twin-rotor combines clean
the fields of barley & sweet corn, their teeth
pressed to the dirt, dust columns rising while,
on television here, some farm boy hauls
to his chest a late Hail Mary. The man
beside me raises his highball Makers
to the screen, the stadium's klieg-lit fans
chanting their rites, the great vegetation
dances of our people—of pep-bands, freshmen
caked in body paint, police—shuddering
into motion again like a corpse. Chris—
the man's name. Which means, in myth, he is
of course a form of shadow self. Second half
vanished at birth. (Basket. Pack of wolves.) We
clink our glasses together. He tells me
he's driven up from Charlotte. He says this
week it is crazy down there, & I know
he means that in Charlotte Tuesday morning
a man—Scott, 43—who waited, neighbors
tell us, for his son school days in the lot
of his apartment complex, was shot—was two
times, in the back once, the chest—in a park
by the city's commissioned. We have seen,
we say, the video. We know the past
a word—*was shot,* in American—gathers
behind it like a train. In Ross once. Cut
in a booth in the back of the Revel Room,
Chicago, the sconces dealing their tongues
of light across the pâtes de fruit, the young
rich of the north side—*the South will . . .* —sipping
their rieslings like peerage. He was holding
a wallet, we agree. Or he raises,
from one angle, almost—is it?—a book. Or
he was holding the hand of his son. No,

of history. Chris, bourbon flashing, asks me
where I was born. *Ohio,* I say—the South
of that place rising like a phoenix. See
it comes back that way. It was midnight. One.
I was four, my father says. The doorbell rang.
& there, you see, was the man's face falling
in on itself like a pumpkin, his insides—so
much it lapped beneath him on the steps. Yes,
there was my father, four kids in the house,
in his left arm my brother—Nicholas
it was, or Eric—in the other the afghan
he wrapped him in, black man my daddy
watched lie down in the front yard & knelt with
til the sheriff showed. It was summertime,
he likes to tell me. The moon shone. I don't
mention this to Chris. Or remember it
really. I remember, of Ohio, hay fields
rippling like a flag. The faces of cows
lifting as we pet them. I remember
Easter the April afterward—plastic eggs
bright in the morning grass, the clacking dimes
& chocolate, a dollar. What did we know
of myth? When God comes back—when Eostre,
that is, or Baldur, when the Christ I loved
once returns—he tows up with him whole fields
of corpses. Sun. Lush cotton. When Sherman
burns Atlanta, he plans his march on crop data
the papers freely publish. The past tense,
you will notice, is seldom used on the tours
of our northern battlefield. We believe,
here, in the present—twelve-pound artillery
lifting its fire from the Peach Orchard, or,
on Round Top, the Texas fifth infantry
pinned down, summer weekends, in the boulders
& tangled roots & backwater. This also
of the present—our Pakistani store clerk's
Honda Civic spray painted *jihadi. All lives*
matter flying from dorm-room windows. One hell
of a landscape, Chris calls it. We toss back
our whiskeys. We are deep, at this point, Chris

& I, in that way men have—a Saturday night,
our tourist town emptied—of opening
up their darknesses to one another. On TV,
the late games are over. It is terrible,
we say, shaking our drunk heads, but also,
listen, he was holding—wasn't he?—some kind
of illicit weapon or other. Or wasn't it
a switchblade? Bomb fuse? A gun? Wasn't, we
are almost certain now, the Howitzer hung
down his pants leg? Yes, we are certain now
in ourselves, the South rising inside us
like a mob, the glossy river of wood
between us—of forgetting, the river, of
fire—unfurling. Above us the bar lights
flicker like stars in their wine glasses. Or that
is what I will think of Sunday morning,
mile six, on South Confederate. The fields
will spread their blanket on the dead. My legs
will turn like pinwheels. I will miss that
when I am ditchweed. It will be so early—
can you hear it?—even the church bells
will be silent. But I should tell you he lived,
that man. In the moonlit yard my father
held water to his mouth. Men came. Later
the parks service will sweep the battlefield
in their pickups. They will gather the flags—
small, prohibited—the faithful furnish
their monuments with. When they are finished
they will dump them in a clearing. Come winter
they burn them again.

Art of Fielding; or, The Night the Turf Tore Open

    & when,
      therefore, with rake
               & walkie-talkie, with television
             cameras circling like attendants, a man
kneeled at the goalline to repair it. Peeled
   back the split carpet—counterfeit
                          pasture—as if
opening a cellar door. As if—

                   In America,
            it was freezing. Ice floes
bobbed in the establishing shots. Outside
        the stadium—overlaid
   with Wendy's ads, Allstate—stone Lincoln
   bridled in his tunic of snow.
                 How magnificent,
though, were we, creators
         of worlds—
                    The refs
sipped Gatorade. Great furnaces
   somewhere pumped out
              their tropic air, ersatz
field flashing its polymers. *All*

    gold, Homer sighs, in delight
           at the shield's fidelity—furrows
turned perfectly black, dragged plow
      lustrous as starlight.
               The idea, dear
sports fans, being that art—Other,
      we are told, to reality—raises it
            nonetheless into spirit. Dear

blind troubadour. Dear Hephaestus—*halting*
   of foot, fallen

three days from Olympus—who in
the forge & bellows of his workshop shows us
dancing. Wedding guests
whirling like flame.

The players,
in replay, in three-
fourths time, tore up
again & again that night the endzone's
lushness. Something
seismic. Small pellets
erupted in their styrene cloud—constellation
of ferns & raptor skeletons, time
with its weight. One man
raked them together. Tacked shut
the hellmouth's seams.

Spirit
of Lincoln. Spirit
of the river as it wakes. One man
ran his fingers through the blades,
like hair. Hovered
close to that earth, as if
he were whispering. It,
beneath him, shivered.

After,

the orchards flowered. The fields
breathed out, like a lung. What
    expectation. After,

at the Peace Fence, veterans
    from North & South swapped belt plates
for the country's press corps. *Country,*

    they whispered, slipping it
across their tongues again as one
    might a finer shiraz. Some regiments

played banjo for their enemies. The president
    was alive still. Sherman
hacked the rice coast into acreage. As in

    forty, with a mule. Imagine. After,
black sheriffs. After, Easter
    as emptied shackles. After,

at supper, the McDonoughs
    of central Pennsylvania looked up
& watched their sheepdog—gone

    two months, a minié ball
bedded in her foreleg—resplendent
    as fable on the porch steps. The moral—*America,*

good puppy. Good
    deathless little dream-fiefdom. If
for a minute . . . If

    in ceremony merely . . . In Manhattan,
after, in lapped serge, Southerners
    marched lockstep, correct

as a stitched line, behind the caskets
        of Union generals. In Virginia,
Lincoln read Shakespeare. Paused,

        we know, at the moment—imagine
the witches prancing, the woods
        risen with their broadswords—sedition

lay chastened & gasping. & after,
        the cotton flourished. Freedmen
practiced their signatures. After, fragments

        of munitions shimmered in their cases
like saints' bones. So bullets,
        for a time, turned vintage. If

in passing, if after
        the worst one country could visit
on a people was visited, history

        dragged its scales to the Southland.
Longstreet—Lee's
        hand at Gettysburg, conductor,

after, of black militias
        in New Orleans—led them,
armed, against a White League

        one would recognize. For which,
afterward, no statues
        were erected. After,

from the ashes . . . After,
        in America, *no masters*
but ourselves the spangled banners

        of schoolkids declared. In Carolina,
after—the exact fairgrounds
        the South had flaunted its stallions

through, or had, of a Sunday, come to
in its veils & worsted—freedmen, wreaths
of lilies in their arms, interred

the Union dead in excelsis. Sweetly,
the mulberries ripened. Worms gathered. After,
we began—

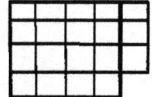

Veterans Day 5K

Then they came forward. From a platform
they waved to their families, Fall Queen
crowning each with corn husks, the color guard
still as monuments. You will want to know
the mayor wore Carhartt. Wept. The runners
halted in their lunges. Flags shirred. Such faith
I will never not long for. My father's
people, these. Who baled a town together
from prayer meetings & diesel fuel. Who,
gone seasons, shoed horses with car tire, tilled
vast acres of cinders. Who dress their deer,
still, like a sacrament. I've signed my name
nowhere. Endured nothing. What is it,
though, that lets a man imagine a country
worth weeping for? Or figure it, for instance,
spring calves climbing to their feet? Evenings
at Sawyer Park—in stirrup pants pitchers
hanging the taut lines of fastballs. That week
they had taken the soybeans off. I thought,
as I ran, road threading the fields, of Greek
reaper gods climbing up through the grottoes
& vents of the underworld. One called Christ
lifted from his cave. Kindred, no, the myths
we've sown the earth with? There was a country,
once, sent its children great distances. Death
lived there. & when they returned—for they did
often—grand races were held, whole parades
marching through farmland, the line of revelers
bright in raiment, bells clapping. Afterward,
the people drank. Their ruler spoke. Go now,
you who have heard, & spread the good news.

Acknowledgments

My sincere gratitude to the following journals, in which poems in this collection originally appeared: *Alaska Quarterly Review:* "'South Will Rise'"; *At Length:* "The Union Forever"; *The Believer:* "Nativity Scene Dedication"; *Beloit Poetry Journal:* "Natinals"; *Boston Review:* "&," "Snow in Inuit," and "Little America"; *Columbia: A Journal of Literature & Art:* "BEACH PARTY STEAK FRY"; *Crazyhorse:* "Good Death" and "Art of Fielding; or, The Night the Turf Tore Open"; *Georgia Review:* "After,"; *Gettysburg Review:* "Michaux State Forest, New Year's"; *Kenyon Review Online:* "Indianapolis 500"; *Likestarlings:* "On Iconoclasm; or, A Little History of Statuary Exploding," "Gapers Delay; or, Mise en Abyme with Fire & Corsage," and "Pro Patria"; *Meridian:* "Veterans Day 5K"; *New England Review:* "Remembrance Day"; *New Ohio Review:* "Local News"; *Pleiades:* "National Anthem" and "Homecoming"; *PLUME:* "Cyclorama."

Thank you, too, to Bill Henderson and the Pushcart Prize staff for reprinting "Michaux State Forest, New Year's" in *Pushcart Prize XLII: Best of the Small Presses* (2018) and to Paisley Rekdal for selecting "After," for *The Best American Poetry 2020*.

•

Thank you to George Bilgere, Eavan Boland, Bill Brown, Christopher Burawa, Jericho Brown, Martha Collins, Tim Dean, John Dudek, Janice N. Harrington, Hugh Martin, Jacques Rancourt, Srikanth Reddy, Philip Metres, David Roderick, Ramón Soto-Crespo, Brian Tierney, and Corey Van Landingham for their invaluable help in revising and re-envisioning this project. Thank you, too, to Kate Barton, Mary Lee Eggart, Laura Gleason, LB Kovac, James Long, Neal Novak, and the anonymous peer reviewer with Louisiana State University Press for their faith in the project, and for their generous work in rounding the manuscript into final form.

This project took shape during a 2016–2017 Emerging Writer Lectureship at Gettysburg College, and owes a significant debt to the faculty and staff who made my time there so meaningful. Thank you especially to Jess Bryant, Mark Drew, Anne and Will Lane, Fred Leebron, Nadine Meyer, Kathryn Rhett, Jody and Mark Rosensteel, and Joyce Topper. This book was also produced with the aid of a 2019 artist's residency at the Gettysburg National Military Park. Thank you to the National Parks Arts Foundation and to the rangers and licensed battlefield guides at Gettysburg—especially David Hamacher, John Krohn, and Zach Siggins—for sharing their wealth of knowledge about the town, the battle, and the monuments there.

•

In researching and thinking about Gettysburg, and about the Civil War generally, I have found a number of texts valuable, especially the following:

Armitage, David. *Civil Wars: A History in Ideas*. New York: Knopf, 2017.

Blight, David W. *Race and Reunion: The Civil War in American Memory*. Cambridge: Harvard UP, 2001.

Blum, Edward J. *Reforging the White Republic: Race, Religion, and American Nationalism, 1865–1898*. Baton Rouge: Louisiana State UP, 2005.

Coates, Ta-Nehisi. "Why Do So Few Blacks Study the Civil War?" *The Atlantic*. November 1, 2017.

Coco, Gregory A. *A Strange and Blighted Land: Gettysburg—The Aftermath of a Battle*. Gettysburg: Thomas Publications, 1995.

Faust, Drew Gilpin. *This Republic of Suffering: Death and the American Civil War*. New York: Vintage, 2008.

Foner, Eric. *Reconstruction: America's Unfinished Revolution 1863–1877*. New York: Harper, 1988.

Foote, Shelby. *The Civil War: A Narrative (Fort Sumter to Perryville)*. New York: Vintage, 1958.

———. *Stars in Their Courses: The Gettysburg Campaign*. New York: The Modern Library, 1994.

Foster, Gaines M. *Ghosts of the Confederacy: Defeat, the Lost Cause, and the Emergence of the New South, 1865–1913*. New York: Oxford UP, 1987.

Franklin, John Hope. *The Militant South 1800–1861*. Cambridge: Harvard UP, 1956.

———. *Reconstruction: After the Civil War*. Chicago: The U of Chicago P, 1961.

Glymph, Thavolia. *Out of the House of Bondage: The Transformation of the Plantation Household*. New York: Cambridge UP, 2008.

Guelzo, Allen C. *Gettysburg: The Last Invasion*. New York: Vintage, 2013.

Harris, M. Keith. *Across the Bloody Chasm: The Culture of Commemoration among Civil War Veterans*. Baton Rouge: Louisiana State UP, 2014.

Sears, Stephen W. *Gettysburg*. New York: Mariner, 2004.

Weeks, Jim. *Gettysburg: Memory, Market, and an American Shrine*. Princeton: Princeton UP, 2003.

Wilson, Charles Reagan. *Baptized in Blood: The Religion of the Lost Cause 1865–1920*. Athens: U of Georgia P, 1980.

Finally, some quotations herein have been slightly edited for sound and rhythm, for which I claim no higher authority than poetic license.

•

"Any understanding of this nation," Shelby Foote has said, "has to be based—and I mean really based—on an understanding of the Civil War." Written in memory of the soldiers and civilians who fought at Gettysburg, this book is an effort toward such understanding.

CPSIA information can be obtained
at www.ICGtesting.com
Printed in the USA
LVHW040435240123
737769LV00004B/766

9 780807 173633